© 2012 Goosebottom Books LLC

Series editor **Shirin Yim Bridges**
Editor **Amy Novesky**
Copy editor **Jennifer Fry**
Editorial assistant **Ann Edwards**
Book design **Jay Mladjenovic**

Typeset in Trajan, Ringbearer, Volkswagen, and Gill Sans
Illustrations rendered in gouache

Manufactured in Malaysia

Library of Congress PCN 2011941874

ISBN: 978-0-9834256-6-3

First Edition 10 9 8 7 6 5 4 3 2 1

Goosebottom Books LLC
710 Portofino Lane, Foster City, CA 94404

www.goosebottombooks.com

The Thinking Girl's Treasury of Dastardly Dames

To my parents, for raising six thinking girls. ~ **Janie Havemeyer**

"THE WARRIOR QUEEN"

Njinga, Queen of Matamba, jumps and leaps as nimbly as a young leopard. A sword dangles from her neck. An axe hugs her hips. Armed with her bow and arrows, she strikes two iron bells. Her army of soldiers surrounds her while her subjects watch, some in awe, others in terror. When she is ready, the warrior queen grabs a broad feather and plunges it through a hole bored through her nose, declaring war on the Portuguese invaders of her kingdom.

Where she lived

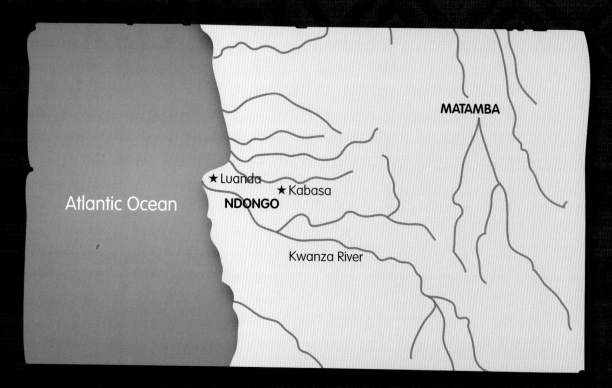

Atlantic Ocean

★ Luanda
NDONGO
★ Kabasa

MATAMBA

Kwanza River

When she lived

This timeline shows when the Dastardly Dames were born.

69 BC	15 AD	1516 AD	1519 AD	1583 AD	1755 AD	1835 AD
Cleopatra	Agrippina	Mary Tudor	Catherine de' Medici	Njinga	Marie Antoinette	Cixi

HER STORY

Njinga was born around 1583, into the royal household of the Ndongo Kingdom of central West Africa. The new princess was named Njinga, which in the Ndongo language means "twist," because she was born with her umbilical cord curled around her neck. After her birth, the soothsayers examined her and shook their heads. "Ayayai!" they cried. This royal baby would not be an easy person.

Njinga grew up with her younger sisters, Mukambu and Kifunji, and her half siblings in the Ndongo capital of Kabasa, a compound of grass-roofed huts decorated with peacock feathers. She was the eldest daughter of Kiluanji, the *ngola*, or king. Her mother was Kiluanji's second wife, a slave woman from another tribe, whom he had fallen in love with when he was just a prince.

During Njinga's childhood, her father was busy fighting a war. Around the time of her birth, settlers from Portugal had established a colony near Ndongo and appointed their own governors to rule it. From the capital city of Luanda, Portuguese merchants bought and sold Africans as slaves to work across the sea in Brazil. While Njinga was growing up, her father regularly left his family to defend his kingdom against Portuguese invasion.

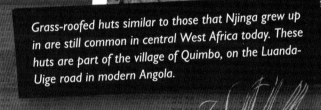

Grass-roofed huts similar to those that Njinga grew up in are still common in central West Africa today. These huts are part of the village of Quimbo, on the Luanda-Uige road in modern Angola.

The slave trade

For many centuries, Africans kept slaves. The slaves were usually prisoners of war or criminals, and were put to work in whatever way their masters wanted. Slaves were bought, inherited, or obtained through raids on neighboring tribes. When the Portuguese arrived, they began to buy slaves to ship to their colonies in the Americas. There, the slaves were sold to work in mines and on plantations. Slave markets were set up across central West Africa so that the Portuguese could buy slaves and ivory in exchange for European trinkets, beads, horses, and Canary wines.

In 1612, a Portuguese trader wrote to the King of Portugal that about ten thousand slaves were being shipped from what is now Angola each year. By the time the Dutch captured the slave port of Luanda in 1641, the estimate hovered between thirteen thousand and sixteen thousand slaves exported each year.

When he wasn't fighting, Kiluanji spent time with Njinga, training her to think like a ruler and fight like a warrior. Even though princesses were not allowed to become ngolas, Njinga's father favored her over her half brother Mbandi. Mbandi, as the eldest son, was heir to the throne, but many thought he was lazy and not as clever as Njinga. Kiluanji hoped that one day his talented daughter Njinga might help Mbandi. Njinga was proud to be the ngola's daughter and ignored anyone who looked down on her for having a slave mother who was not from Ndongo.

As she grew up, Njinga practiced all that her father taught her, probably hoping at times that her father would leave her in charge instead of Mbandi. As a young princess tucked away safely in Kabasa, Njinga was protected from the war raging on the outskirts of Ndongo. She had a relatively easy life and, in time, married and gave birth to a son. But when her father died, leaving Mbandi in charge, Njinga's whole life changed as swiftly as sails in the wind.

Mbandi was suspicious and insecure. He saw enemies within the ranks of his own family. First, Njinga's younger half brother mysteriously died, then, her only son. Rumors spread that Mbandi had them killed. The royal household had become a dangerous place. Njinga fled from Kabasa with her sisters, the only siblings she trusted and loved.

While Njinga was in exile, the Portuguese spread into the Ndongo kingdom like army ants. They built a fort near Kabasa and enlisted the help of a fierce warrior band called the Imbangala. The Imbangala ate human flesh and loved to drink palm wine. Now, these cannibals invaded Ndongo, capturing thousands as slaves for the Portuguese, and killing and eating others. Twice they sacked Kabasa, capturing Mbandi's mother and wives. Finally, Mbandi was forced to flee when Kabasa was burned to the ground. He escaped to the Kindonga Islands in the Kwanza River, where Njinga eventually joined him. She decided to put her bad feelings for Mbandi aside, realizing her kingdom needed her.

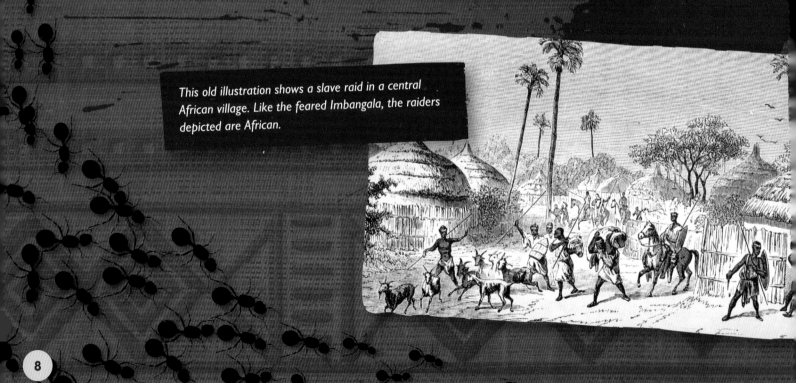

This old illustration shows a slave raid in a central African village. Like the feared Imbangala, the raiders depicted are African.

When a Portuguese ship arrived at the bustling slave port of Luanda bringing a new governor, Joao Correia de Sousa, Njinga saw an opportunity to help her country and her brother. Mbandi asked her to visit the governor as his ambassador to negotiate a peace treaty, and Njinga agreed. After all, she spoke Portuguese and was a clever debater.

In the fifteenth century, the Portuguese developed the carrack, three- or four-masted ships that were sturdy enough for long ocean voyages, and large enough to hold provisions and merchandise. These ships allowed the Portuguese to travel great distances, from Europe to Asia, Africa, and the Americas. This painting dates from around 1540, just over forty years before Njinga was born.

For this important mission, the princess gathered a military escort, a handful of trusted servants, and her two sisters. To impress the governor and remind him of her royal status, she traveled to Luanda on a litter carried by four strong porters, reclining against colorful pillows. Musicians blowing ivory horns, ringing bells, and rattling calabashes would have accompanied her too, as this was a royal procession.

At the governor's fortress, Njinga marched into the stone reception room, but immediately noticed that something was not right. The governor was sitting on a regal chair, but there was no seat for her, except a cushion on the floor. Proud Njinga quickly thought of a solution. She ordered her servant to form a human chair so that she could sit on her servant's back and speak with the governor on an equal footing. Looking right into the eyes of the haughty man, she explained, "I represent a sovereign people, and I am ready to continue this conversation only on that basis."

Njinga bargained skillfully with the governor. If the Portuguese would leave Ndongo, drive the Imbangala out of the region, return Ndongo slaves, and restore Mbandi's throne, Njinga promised to supply war captives from rival tribes for the slave trade. The greedy governor was persuaded to make peace with the Kingdom of Ndongo when Njinga made him this offer of slaves.

This engraving shows European slave traders mustering slaves, while a ship waits for its human cargo offshore.

Once the terms of the peace treaty had been settled, Njinga thought of a way to twist her new alliance to suit her own ambitions. Her weak-kneed brother had almost destroyed her family's kingdom. It was time she took charge. Even though she was a woman, she believed that the governor would support her as the next ngola if she became a Catholic. So, she decided to be baptized in Luanda and was christened Dona Ana de Sousa in honor of Governor de Sousa. He became her godfather. Njinga had taken a critical step toward becoming the first female ngola, but she still had to deal with Mbandi.

This engraving of Njinga's baptism was based on a watercolor made by Giovanni Cavazzi, a Catholic missionary working in central West Africa. It is unlikely that Cavazzi witnessed Njinga's baptism himself, although he was probably working in the area around the time that she died. The engraving was published in a book about his travels in 1687, twenty-four years after Njinga's death.

While Njinga waited for the governor to drive the Imbangala out of Ndongo and send his own soldiers back to Luanda, Mbandi mysteriously died. Had Mbandi ended his own life? Or was Njinga involved? Most people believed that she had poisoned her half brother. Either way, since Mbandi's son was too young to rule, the governor supported Njinga—now his Catholic ally—as the *regent*, or acting ruler, of Ndongo. Njinga's dream of becoming ngola seemed within reach.

Once again, the people of Ndongo had a strong ruler. Even if Njinga did not hold the title of ngola yet, she was in charge, and unlike Mbandi before her, she refused to let the Portuguese boss her around. If the governor demanded that she return Portuguese prisoners, she would demand he return African slaves from Brazil. If the governor didn't treat her as an equal, she would fight back. Njinga began to persuade slave soldiers of the Portuguese army to desert. She offered them land and freedom in exchange for their allegiance. "Be lords of your own lands rather than Portuguese captives!" she cried. Soon, the Portuguese realized that Njinga was not a puppet ruler after all; the ranks of their armies were shrinking by the thousands, while Njinga's army was growing.

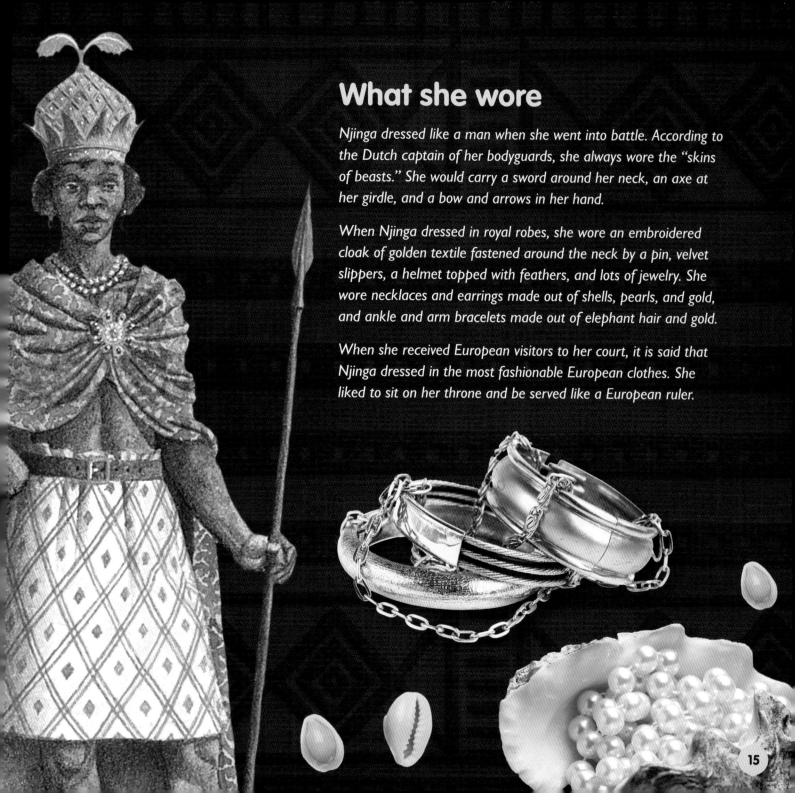

What she wore

Njinga dressed like a man when she went into battle. According to the Dutch captain of her bodyguards, she always wore the "skins of beasts." She would carry a sword around her neck, an axe at her girdle, and a bow and arrows in her hand.

When Njinga dressed in royal robes, she wore an embroidered cloak of golden textile fastened around the neck by a pin, velvet slippers, a helmet topped with feathers, and lots of jewelry. She wore necklaces and earrings made out of shells, pearls, and gold, and ankle and arm bracelets made out of elephant hair and gold.

When she received European visitors to her court, it is said that Njinga dressed in the most fashionable European clothes. She liked to sit on her throne and be served like a European ruler.

What she ate

Njinga was accused of eating her nephew's heart and being a cannibal after she joined the Imbangala. Her normal diet, however, would have been that of the people of Ndongo: meat from birds, hares, rats, snakes, hippopotami, and crocodiles. They raised chickens and dogs that would be eaten too. They grew beans, yams, and radishes, and ate bananas. Eggs, honey, and kola nuts were considered delicacies. Daily markets were held to trade goods, and the currency used was rock salt. Three blocks of salt might buy a goat, for instance.

After she became Queen of Matamba, Njinga always ate in public, sitting on a mat where she could receive her people. She ate with her hands and would tear off small pieces of meat to share with her attendants and soldiers. When she was finished eating, her attendants were allowed to eat her leftovers. Eighty different dishes might be served at one meal.

Njinga loved drinking wine, both the locally made palm wine and imported European wines. A barrel of imported Canary wine might cost her one slave. When Njinga drank, the people around her clapped their hands and snapped their fingers together. They also touched their fingers to their feet as a sign that the queen should enjoy her beverage from her head to her toes.

From Njinga's capital on the Kindonga Islands, she began to spread stories about the evil ways of the Portuguese. Governor Sousa had never followed through on his promises to her. Moving like a tidal wave across the land, Njinga's words stirred people. She appealed to African kings and chiefs. As her power and popularity grew, Njinga decided the time had come to become Ngola of Ndongo. But now she had to figure out what to do about her nephew, Mbandi's heir to the throne.

She sent presents to her nephew's guardian, Kaza, who had been sheltering the young prince for years. Kaza, bewitched by Njinga's good looks, agreed to return the boy in exchange for her promise to marry him. But once the boy was handed over, he was apparently murdered. Many whispered that Njinga had killed him and feasted on his heart. When the Portuguese heard these stories, they declared war on Njinga. They appointed a new ruler for Ndongo, someone they knew would do whatever they wanted.

But Njinga was not about to give in. She tried to convince her people to support her claim to the throne. Although many of her subjects did not like the new ngola, they still did not believe a woman should rule their kingdom. So Njinga gave her husband the title of ngola, hoping to rule as their queen. When this didn't work, she began to dress like a man and forced her husband to dress like a woman. Finally, she renounced her Catholic name and proclaimed herself ngola.

For three years, Njinga fought the Portuguese forces and their puppet ruler from her stronghold on the Kindonga Islands, until one day they attacked her island refuge, capturing most of her family, including her sisters. Njinga and a few hundred followers escaped by rappelling down ropes along rocky cliffs. With most of her army scattered, Njinga fled eastward to a camp of the hated Imbangala. How far would she go to win back her kingdom?

The kingdom of Ndongo was not the flat, spreading African plain of popular imagination. It was made up of forests, grasslands, rivers, hills, valleys—and dramatic cliffs like these around twenty miles south of Luanda. Njinga may have rappelled down something very similar!

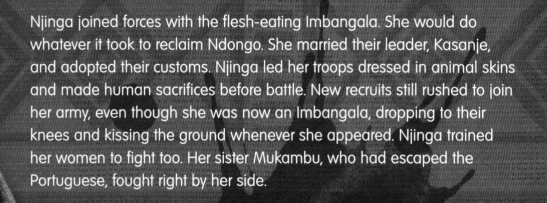

Njinga joined forces with the flesh-eating Imbangala. She would do whatever it took to reclaim Ndongo. She married their leader, Kasanje, and adopted their customs. Njinga led her troops dressed in animal skins and made human sacrifices before battle. New recruits still rushed to join her army, even though she was now an Imbangala, dropping to their knees and kissing the ground whenever she appeared. Njinga trained her women to fight too. Her sister Mukambu, who had escaped the Portuguese, fought right by her side.

The Imbangala

The Imbangala were independent armies who lived in fortified camps and roamed across central West Africa invading, attacking, and destroying. They filled everyone with fear and dread. They practiced infanticide (the killing of babies) and ate human flesh, often consuming the remains of their victims or making human sacrifices before going into battle. The Portuguese used some Imbangala bands to bring them slaves. The Imbangala provided the Portuguese with thousands of captives.

Njinga won some battles against the Portuguese, but lost others. Forced to retreat farther into the outskirts of her kingdom, Njinga broke away from Kasanje and led her people over the forested hills, plains, and rivers to the highlands of Matamba. Discovering that the King of Matamba had died, Njinga captured his daughter and appointed herself Queen of Matamba.

Njinga continued to fight the Portuguese for decades, getting help from the Dutch, but she never succeeded in forcing them out of her country. They captured her sister Mukambu again and drowned her sister Kifunji in the Kwanza River.

Eventually, Njinga retreated to the hills of her Matamba kingdom. She was in her sixties, as old as the crocodiles on the banks of the Kwanza River. She had lost a kingdom, a son, and a sister. How could she lose Mukambu too? Njinga decided the time had come to make peace with the Portuguese. She agreed to give up her Imbangala customs, settle down, and stop fighting. She exchanged more than one hundred slaves for the release of Mukambu.

For a few more years, Njinga, Queen of Matamba, coexisted peacefully with her enemies, always insisting they treat her as their equal. She had saved her surviving sister's life and arranged for her to become the next monarch of Matamba. She had lost Ndongo, but she had built another powerful kingdom of refugees, uniting many kingdoms and tribes in her struggle. She had never lost her determination to be free.

Njinga died one winter day in 1663. Her people dressed her in royal robes studded with precious stones and slipped velvet shoes on her feet. They placed a bow and arrows in her hands and covered her with flowers. One hundred warriors played music while her body was carried into the courtyard of her compound. A crowd of mourners gazed upon their famous warrior queen with pride and wept.

The funeral of Queen Njinga. An engraving based on a watercolor by the missionary Giovanni Cavazzi, 1687.

After her death, the Portuguese advanced into the lands of central West Africa like wildfire and the slave trade increased. It would take more than three hundred years for Njinga's dreams of freedom to finally come true. In 1975, her descendants gained independence from the Portuguese and the People's Republic of Angola was born. Warrior Queen Njinga had been their inspiration.

How dastardly was she?

Njinga was accused of many murders—among other dreadful things. Was she really so dastardly?

Accusation	Defense
Murdering her half brother and her nephew, and eating her nephew's heart.	There is no reliable evidence that Njinga was responsible for these deaths. Since our sources are mainly reports from the Portuguese, who wanted to cast her as the villain, using the supposed murder of her nephew as their excuse to appoint their own ngola and declare war, it seems likely that these stories were exaggerated. In fact, some reports say that Njinga's brother ended his own life by swallowing poison.
Trading in slaves with the Portuguese.	Slavery was common in Africa in Njinga's day. Even her own mother had been a slave. Njinga fought all her life to protect and release her own people from slavery, but she happily traded in slaves who were criminals or captives of war from other tribes.
Sacrificing humans before battle and killing babies at birth.	When Njinga joined the Imbangala in an effort to expel the Portuguese from her country, she adopted their customs. This did include human sacrifice and infanticide.

Bibliography

Birmingham, David. *Trade and Conflict in Angola—The Mbundu and Their Neighbors Under the Influence of the Portuguese 1483-1790*. Clarendon Press, 1966.

Clarke, John Henrik. "African Warrior Queens." In *Black Women in Antiquity*, edited by Ivan Van Sertima, 123-134. Transaction Publishers, 1992.

Diouf, Sylviane Anna. *Kings and Queens of Southern Africa*. Franklin Watts, 2000.

Fraser, Antonia. *The Warrior Queens—The Legends and the Lives of the Women Who Have Led Their Nations in War*. Anchor Books, 2004.

Hansen, Joyce. *African Princess—The Amazing Lives of Africa's Royal Women*. Hyperion Books for Children, 2004.

Heywood, Linda M., and John K. Thornton. *Central Africans, Atlantic Creoles, and the Foundation of the Americas, 1585-1660*. Cambridge University Press, 2007.

Riedinger, Edward A. "Njinga." http://salempress.com/store/samples/great_lives_from_history_seventeenth/great_lives_from_history_seventeenth_njinga.htm.

Schwarz-Bart, Simone with Andre Schwartz-Bart. *In Praise of Black Women: Ancient African Queens*. The University of Wisconsin Press, 2001.

Seligson, Susan. "The Enduring Power of Queen Njinga." *Bostonia* (Winter Spring 2011): http://www.bu.edu/bostonia/winter-spring11/queen/.

Sweetman, David. *Women Leaders in African History*. Heinemann, 1984.

Thomas, Hugh. *The Slave Trade: The Story of the Atlantic Slave Trade: 1440-1870*. Simon & Schuster, 1999.